The Little Book That Moves Mountains

By Derek Schneider

Derek Schneider
The Little Book That Moves Mountains

©2023 Derek Schneider
ISBN 979-8504-9082-29

.

Cover and interior design by Golden Truth Publishing
Kyiv, Ukraine. All rights reserved
publish@goldentruth.pro
www.goldentruth.pro

Contents

Foreword

«Derek Schneider has captured God's heart for us to be completely whole in spirit, soul and body in this amazing book. He shares how, throughout many years of ministry, he has seen countless people set free from the bondage of pain and sickness. Seeing them made whole by the power of God has impacted not only those who have been healed, but has been a living demonstration of the overwhelming love of God for people!

The Little Book that Moves Mountains is one of the most refreshing books I have come across in some time. This is a book that simply and beautifully gathers the scriptures that pertain to healing and puts them in one place. As you read it, you will understand the simple truth of healing: It is God who heals. And you will see through this powerful little book what the healer says about your healing!"

Stacey Campbell

Introduction

Still, to this day, one of my most favourite scriptures in entire bible would have to be **2 Peter 1:3-4** which reads...

"³Seeing that His divine power has granted to us everything pertaining to life and godliness, through the true knowledge of Him who called us by His own glory and excellence. ⁴For by these He has granted to us His precious and magnificent promises, so that by them you may become partakers of the divine nature, having escaped the corruption that is in the world by lust" (NASB).

For many, the highlight of a passage like this would be the fact that we, as believers, are able to access the precious promises of God because of our faith in Jesus Christ. Promises such as various healings, prosperity (both financial and other), blessings on our homes and families, and virtually anything that we would deem as being a blessing from God to us. Sometimes we make the mistake of seeking blessings of God more than we seek knowing God, who is our greatest treasure. Still, He desires for us to walk in all of these promises as we pursue in the intimate knowledge of Jesus Christ. This is one of the reasons why I have created *The Little Book That Moves Mountains*. God *does* heal today. He *does* perform miracles to them that believe. His infinite mercy even performs miracles even for those who do not yet believe.

As I read a passage like the one above, I celebrate the fact that I have access to these gifts and promises, and they are absolutely free! However, the high point of this passage for me personally would be the awesome and mysterious fact that we actually can be *"partakers of the divine nature"*. To me, this is something greater altogether. The fact that we as believers, through Jesus Christ, also have the ability to partake of the very NATURE of God - His attributes, His characteristics, and His wonderful virtues - is the greatest miracle of all!

Essentially, salvation is much more than an invitation for a free ride to heaven. It is, in fact, an invitation to be restored back to God's very *"image and likeness"* **(Gen. 1:26)**. As we seek to become like Him and to partake of His nature at the expense of our own, these precious promises become ours. Whether we are facing a difficult physical ailment that has literally crippled us or the financial crisis that makes us wonder if our next meal will literally have to be delivered by the angels themselves, we have access to all the power that we need. This is not only because of the fact that we believe it is possible for God to come through for us, but also because His Word has literally *"become flesh"* in us (according to **John 1:14**) and brings forth the fruit of our Master, Jesus.

The idea of being a *"partaker of the divine nature"* or the *"Word becoming flesh in us"* is far more than receiving a *"free hand-out"* from heaven because we read that it is possible. No! Rather, it is a literal transformation within us because His words are *"spirit and life"* **(John 6:63)**. It is the idea that we can follow after the model used by God when His very *"Word"* became *"flesh"* and *"dwelt among us"* and *"we saw His glory" (John 1:14).* This Word (of course we know it is Jesus) literally took on flesh so as to become the very express image of God in order to display what the invisible God looks like, according to image and likeness. We could actually behold Him, handle Him, hear Him, and understand Him - we could see the glory of God in the Word becoming flesh. All of God's abilities, nature, and, of course, virtue, took on a flesh suit in the form of God's Son, Jesus Christ. What a powerful model for us to attain to! Jesus essentially revealed God to the world through becoming the very image of God and God's Word manifested in flesh and blood.

We can probably say that this is the reason for the success we see in the life of Jesus, not only in the area of His sinlessness, but also in His divine power to perform miracles. If God's Word says, *"I, the Lord am your healer" (Exodus 15:26),* then surely Jesus embodied that Word to the degree that those who came needing healing received their healing *(Matthew 8:16).* If God the Father is full of love and is love, *(1 John 4:8)* and is the Creator and establisher of what we know to be the *"fruit of the spirit" (Galatians 5:22-23)*, then surely Jesus Christ perfected what that looks like in the human life. What an awesome example for us! Oh, that we could make God's Word become flesh in us and bear, not only the nature and image of God to the world, but also be able to have biblical results in our ministries, families, and day-to-day lives!

Without a doubt we have a great *"treasure in earthen vessels" (2 Corinthians 4:7)*; a great key to being able to accomplish what God would accomplish on earth if He were here, so to speak. My friends, this is found in our ability to make the Word become flesh. It is then that we will see God's results through us!

My Story...

A number of years ago I had an encounter with the Lord that completely transformed my life. It caused me to leave my career path at the time and enter into full time ministry in a radical way. I had been raised in the church, but was running from the Lord and His calling for my life, and I was pursuing a music career that was quickly becoming successful. In the Lord's mercy, just before I was to sign a recording contract, He visited me one night and called me into full-time ministry. I surrendered! A few weeks later, after a meeting with my manager and others, I finally quit the music business for good. I made a *'deal with God.'*

After the meeting, as I drove home, I had tears streaming down my face. I told the Lord (as if I had the power to do that; I'm sure He merely entertained me) *"if I give all of this music stuff up, you better not make me a 'cold preacher.' I want signs and wonders happening in my ministry - real power!"* As audacious as that sounds, I made this statement with a pure and soft heart, and I think He understood that.

Throughout my life, my issue with the church had been that a lot of what I read about in the Bible (more specifically the New Testament) seemed to seldom happen through us beyond the four walls of the church, let alone in the church. Yet, we seemed to celebrate every

Sunday morning as though it was! I could not understand this. We would quote the various faith, healing, and miracle scriptures, and occasionally work up the nerve to actually *'lay hands on the sick.'* Our prayers, at times, seemed powerless and religious. I am sad to say, many times I walked away wondering why we pray like this. Why we get so excited when we rarely see the result that is promised in God's Word. After being in this kind of environment for a while, I naturally became religious, unbelieving, and I even began to doubt the power of God altogether in the area of *"signs and wonders following"* *(Mark 16: 17-18).*

Following my '*deal with God*,' I made it my priority to see the bible come alive in me and through me regardless of what the sceptics had to say. I was so convinced that what was promised in the Bible IS possible for today and, in my simple faith, I decided to find all of the healing and miracle scriptures I could. I read them as often as I could and I started praying for every sick person I could! During that time I spent a lot of money buying tapes and books from TV evangelists as well.

Looking back on this pursuit now, after ten years have passed, I am not actually sure what my real motivation was at the time - whether it was to reveal God's love or just to prove something. Whatever it was, I was on a mission to make the Word, as it pertains to faith, healing, and miracles, become *"flesh"* in me.

Every day I would search the New Testament looking for scriptures on the subject, and if I saw someone in an arm brace, a wheel chair, or even suffering from a common cold, I prayed for them, whether they were in the church or on the street! My pursuit began well and I was confident that God honours His Word, just as I had been taught. Yet, somehow, after a few months I found myself caught in the same cycle that I had grown up in - of knowing how to quote *"these signs shall follow those who believe" (Mark 16:17-18)*, but not actually seeing any signs follow me! It is not to say that no one benefitted in any way from my prayers at that time, but I definitely wasn't seeing the outpouring as described in the book of Acts!

This problem mystified me. I am sure that many who have come to this road block have found themselves frustrated in the same way I was, and turned back as I had using the excuse, *"Who can know the ways of the Lord or can understand why He DIDN'T deliver?"* For me, that just wasn't an option anymore. Truthfully, I had fallen in love with Jesus, and I knew in my heart that His Bible is true. Yet, on the more carnal, honest side, I had given up a music career for this, and I wanted results! Whether it was the leading of the Spirit or just my stubborn drive to get this Bible active in my life, the lack of the miraculous literally drove me into extended periods of prayer and seeking God's face - that was just what He wanted.

How to Use This Book...

The Little Book that Moves Mountains is a compilation of the scriptures that pertain to faith, healing, the miraculous, signs and wonders, authority over demons, and the power of God. These scriptures have been put together in one easy to read, and easy to carry 'small book.' It is my desire for you to be able to carry this book with you daily and, whenever time permits, to be able to pull it out and memorize, meditate on, and pray these scriptures until they take root in you that you might manifest God's glory wherever you go.

It is also my desire for people to be able to have these read out loud while praying for the sick, the demonized, or anyone in need of a miracle. You will notice that just reading through these daily (at one point in my life I was reading all of them a few times per week) your faith will not only increase, but in moments of great need the Holy Spirit will quicken these to your minds and you will pray with faith and fervency and literally apprehend these promises as a partaker of the divine nature! You will discover that truly NOTHING will be impossible for you as you step into the realm of *"if you ask anything in my name" (John 16:23)*. You will sense the closeness of God and feel His authority come alive in you. You will have a revelation of your authority on earth as an extension of God to execute His divine purposes. Even now, as I write this, I feel that faith - the faith that lays a demand on heaven to fulfill the promises of God's word. I pray that as you labour on these scriptures and as you cause the words of our Lord to *"become flesh"* in you, that you will truly partake of the divine nature, God's promises, and that you will truly *"move mountains!"* God bless you.

We are called to greatness!

Pastor Derek Schneider

Personal Testimony of Healing

One evening, in April of 2011, I doubled over with intense stomach pain. The pain was actually so severe that I felt I only had a few minutes to alert someone. I went to my parents room, woke them up falling into their bed, I passed out and had a seizure. When I woke up, my mom was on the phone with 911. Within a few minutes the paramedics arrived and took me, barely coherent, to the hospital. When I got to the hospital, the doctor ordered several tests – which all came out strangely clear. With the pain having now subsided, they sent me home and told me to see my family doctor for further testing. While they did not know what had caused this traumatic experience, they explained that the seizure was likely a result of the intense pain. Although the side of my body was subtly still feeling the effects of the traumatic experience, the pain had significantly decreased, so I assumed the whole ordeal was over. Little did I realize this was actually the beginning of three very difficult weeks?

The days that followed, I began to struggle a lot with stomach pain, weakness and fatigue. It actually got to the point where any movement, at all, brought on severe stomach pain. Even the smallest activities left me feeling very uncomfortable. Also, the never knowing when another pain attack could come brought on a lot of anxiety and I was soon feeling *held captive* by this situation. Eating solid food would trigger the pain and discomfort, so I ate very little. Because I didn't have any energy, I stayed in bed a lot, hoping the rest would help me recover. I was not able to go to work. I prayed a lot, asking God to protect me and reveal the source of the problem so that it could be treated, and I could recover and get back to my job and ministry, which had just begun to grow significantly. I saw my family doctor a few times, as I was instructed, but no one seemed to have any answers for me, except performing more tests. I had several pain attacks, like the first one, but still had no answers. The extreme pain, and attacks continued and I felt it was time my pastor and friends were notified.

Coincidently (or not), at the time this all occurred, I was preparing a 25 week recovery program designed to rehabilitate women who have suffered through childhood sexual abuse. In addition to developing this program, I was also overseeing the preparation of a ground breaking new discipleship training for our young adults – the launch was only a few weeks away. I was very concerned that I wouldn't be well enough to pull it off. Many had already spent money and registered for the program and arrangements had been made.

Two weeks passed, and I was getting worse. I could barely eat any food. My family doctor instructed me to go to the hospital if I got any worse. A few more days passed by and I began to vomit uncontrollably. My parents took me back to the hospital. While waiting for assistance, I passed out twice from the pain. The hospital kept me overnight to treat me with pain medication and high doses of antibiotics through intravenous because I was not able to keep anything down anymore. Again, more tests were ordered. I spent the next 24 hours at the hospital hoping to find relief but still received no answers. I saw a stomach specialist who mentioned to me that it was possible I was suffering with pancreatitis, but I was not able to receive a diagnosis because they couldn't catch it in the testing. I was given a requisition with instructions on what to do if I experienced another attack and was sent home again. I was instructed to stay on a liquid diet until they were able to come to some conclusion. At this point, I was feeling anxious. I never knew when I would get these attacks or how bad it was going to be. With the program and other ministry obligations looming over my head, the stress of all of this became unbearable and I knew only God could be my answer!

I was on a liquid diet for 8 days. This did help some, but I still struggled with tenderness and pressure in my stomach that left me feeling very uncomfortable. Pastor Derek Schneider was holding an anointing service at The Embassy Church – the emphasis was on signs, wonders and miracles. I decided to attend the service even though I was not really in the shape to do so. I made arrangements to be picked up early if I had any problems.

That night Pastor Derek preached a powerful message and the Holy Spirit was moving in a powerful way during the ministry time. Many were touched. The leaders of the young adult ministry were asked to pray for people, so, as a leader in this ministry, I began to pray for people. Even though I was in a lot of pain, I was excited to see people being set free of bondages. As the night continued, the presence of the Holy Spirit became stronger and stronger. As soon as it looked like Pastor Derek was about to close the service, I called for someone to pick me up and take me home. Just as I was walking slowly out of the auditorium, Pastor Derek called me back so that he could pray specifically for me.

As he began to pray, he quickly handed his Bible to one of the young adult women. He asked her to read all of the healing scriptures highlighted in his New Testament. Taking the microphone, she began reading out of the Book of John. Pastor Derek laid hands on me, as she read, and the congregation gathered around me in agreement. For several minutes he prayed as the young woman, holding the Bible continued to read aloud the healing scriptures – one after another. I could feel my faith rising as I identified with the stories of sick people approaching Jesus. When she began reading the verses about Lazarus being raised from the dead *(John 11)*, I physically felt a stirring happening on the inside of my stomach. Immediately the pressure released and the tension in my stomach relieved. I could literally feel the Word come alive on the inside, becoming life within me, causing my body to come into order. When she read that they *"loosed the bindings from Lazarus"* after he came out of the tomb, I felt the healing complete. Instantly, the tenderness was gone – before this even to touch my side resulted in terrible pain. The swelling left and ALL the pain was gone. My energy returned and I felt completely fine.

After Pastor Derek prayed, we began to worship and praise. I danced a bit and moved my body around in ways I wasn't able to before this and it proved to me that the healing had taken place. Before I left the service, I was feeling hungry. I went home and ate dinner – it was the first full meal I had eaten in weeks. There was absolutely no more pain.

That night I had an incredible sleep - one of the best sleeps that I can remember! The next day I went back to work. I didn't need any recuperation time. Immediately, I was well and there was no evidence that I had even been sick. By this I knew a true miracle had taken place! I also experienced something like acceleration in time - in that the time I had lost sick and was unable to prepare for the training, I was still able to complete all the administration a week in advance. The discipleship training went smoothly with no interruptions. I excitedly went to see my specialist and he confirmed that my stomach was fine and there were no problems whatsoever. This was a demonstration of the power of the Word mixed with faith. I truly experienced the Word of God *"becoming flesh"*.

Personal Testimony

by Danielle Boddy

Miracle Testimony

My name is Josephine Ansing, and I suffered from stage 2 cervical cancer for 11 months, when I received healing prayer from Pastor Derek Schneider.

I had begun chemo and radiation treatments, but unfortunately they were not working and the cancer was not reducing. Plus, these treatments caused all kinds of other terrible symptoms and effects. I am a mother and wife, and the thought of losing my life and not watching my 6 children grow up, had me in crippling constant fear.

One day my nephew invited me and my family to their home to meet Pastor Derek, who happened to be staying there having just married his wife Sarah (my nephew's sister in law). I was told that Pastor Derek had a unique gift of healing and he had been asked to pray for me right there in the family home. I believed in the power of Jesus, although had never been healed of anything before. I was desperate, and thankful that someone would care enough even to pray for me. I wanted all the prayer I could get.

I remember Pastor Derek coming into the room and asking a few questions and then proceeded to pray for me. He told me to place my hand on my lower abdomen and he asked his wife to place her hand over mine. I immediately began to feel something and it only increased as the session of prayer continued. I began to feel something and my husband began to weep for some reason. After Pastor Derek finished the prayer time, I felt as though a big weight had been lifted off of me. I still didn't know what to expect but I was believing Jesus for a miracle. To my amazement (and to everyone's amazement still to this very day) shortly after this prayer encounter, I went to the washroom and passed the cancerous tumour into the toilet! What a miracle!

After visiting the doctor, I was able to get confirmation that this really was a tumour that had left my body! Just to be on the safe side, and just in case there was any cancerous cells left behind, the doctor encouraged me to finish up my treatments. Here is where this miracle testimony gets even better. While completing my chemo and radiation treatments, I did not seem to have those terrible side effects that are normal for cancer treatment. I had no tiredness, in fact I felt some kind of great energy! I can only attribute this to the power of God, and I want to praise Jesus for healing me and giving me my life back. I am totally healed!

Josephine Ansing

Healing
Scriptures

Faith

As we embark on this sacred exploration of Faith, we immerse ourselves in the profound wisdom and enlightenment found in the holy scriptures. They guide us towards understanding and appreciating the power of unyielding belief in the divine. A belief that bridges the gap between the temporal and the eternal, the visible and the unseen.

Drawing from the Gospel of Matthew, we encounter numerous instances demonstrating how faith, paired with an unfaltering conviction in God's abilities, orchestrates miraculous healings. Time and again, Jesus reaffirms, «Your faith has made you well.» In the realm of the divine, physical ailments cease to be barriers as faith unlocks the door to healing and wholeness. It shows us that faith is not merely a notion, but an active, vibrant, and transformative power.

In the words of Paul, in his letters to the Romans and Corinthians, we find that faith is born from hearing the word of God and is fostered through a spirit of unwavering belief, even when our human sight fails us. This unseen, enduring, and timeless power of faith offers the shield that extinguishes the flaming arrows of the evil one, and allows us to fight the good fight, as exhorted by Paul to Timothy.

This exploration through the labyrinth of scriptures underpins our journey through faith's intricate path and prepares us to delve deeper into this compelling element of spiritual life. It is a journey of discovery, revelation, and ultimately, transformation.

Matthew 8:2-3 ~ [2]And behold, a leper came to Him, and bowed down to Him, saying, «Lord, if You are willing, You can make me clean.» [3]And He stretched out His hand and touched him, saying, «I am willing; be cleansed.» And immediately his leprosy was cleansed.

Matthew 8:5-10, 13 ~[5]And when He had entered Capernaum, a centurion came to Him, entreating Him, [6]and saying, "Lord, my servant is lying paralyzed at home, suffering great pain." [7]And He said to him, «I will come and heal him.» [8]But the centurion answered and said, «Lord, I am not worthy for You to come under my roof, but just say the word, and my servant will be healed. [9]»For I, too, am a man under authority, with soldiers under me; and I say to this one, 'Go!' and he goes, and to another, 'Come!' and he comes, and to my slave, 'Do this!' and he does it.» [10]Now when Jesus heard this, He marvelled, and said to those who were following, "Truly I say to you, I have not found such great faith with anyone in Israel."... [13]And Jesus said to the centurion, "Go your way; let it be done to you as you have believed." And the servant was healed that very hour.

Matthew 9:20-22 ~²⁰And behold, a woman who had been suffering from a hemorrhage for twelve years, came up behind Him and touched the fringe of His cloak; ²¹for she was saying to herself, «If I only touch His garment, I shall get well.» ²²But Jesus turning and seeing her said, «Daughter, take courage; your faith has made you well.» And at once the woman was made well.

Matthew 9:27-30a ~²⁷And as Jesus passed on from there, two blind men followed Him, crying out, and saying, "Have mercy on us, Son of David!" ²⁸And after He had come into the house, the blind men came up to Him, and Jesus said to them, «Do you believe that I am able to do this?» They said to Him, «Yes, Lord.» ²⁹Then He touched their eyes, saying, «Be it done to you according to your faith.» ³⁰And their eyes were opened.

Matthew 15:22-28 ~ ²²And behold, a Canaanite woman came out from that region, and began to cry out, saying, "Have mercy on me, O Lord, Son of David; my daughter is cruelly demon-possessed." ²³But He did not answer her a word. And His disciples came to Him and kept asking Him, saying, "Send her away, for she is shouting out after us." ²⁴But He answered and said, "I was sent only to the lost sheep of the house of Israel." ²⁵ But she came and began to bow down before Him, saying, "Lord, help me!" [26] And He answered and said, "It is not good to take the children's bread and throw it to the dogs." [27]But she said, "Yes, Lord; but even the dogs feed on the crumbs, which fall from their masters' table." [28]Then Jesus answered and said to her, "O woman, your faith is great; be it done for you as you wish." And her daughter was healed at once.

Matthew 19:26 ~ And looking upon them Jesus said to them, «With men this is impossible, but with God all things are possible.»

Matthew 21:21-22 ~ [21]And Jesus answered and said to them, «Truly I say to you, if you have faith and do not doubt, you shall not only do what was done to the fig tree, but even if you say to this mountain, 'Be taken up and cast into the sea,' it shall happen. [22]»And all things you ask in prayer, believing, you shall receive.»

Mark 5:25-30,34 ~ [25]And a woman who had had a hemorrhage for twelve years, [26]and had endured much at the hands of many physicians, and had spent all that she had and was not helped at all, but rather had grown worse, [27]after hearing about Jesus, came up in the crowd behind Him, and touched His cloak. [28]For she thought, «If I just touch His garments, I shall get well.» [29]And immediately the flow of her blood was dried up; and she felt in her body that she was healed of her affliction. [30]And immediately Jesus, perceiving in Himself that the power proceeding from Him had gone forth, turned around in the crowd and said, «Who touched My garments?»... [34]And He said to her, «Daughter, your faith has made you well; go in peace, and be healed of your affliction.»

Mark 6:5-6a ~ [5]And He could do no miracle there except that He laid His hands upon a few sick people and healed them. [6]And He wondered at their unbelief.

Mark 10:27 ~ Looking upon them, Jesus said, «With men it is impossible, but not with God; for all things are possible with God.»

Mark 10:51-52 ~ [51]And answering him, Jesus said, «What do you want Me to do for you?» And the blind man said to Him, «Rabboni, I want to regain my sight!» [52]And Jesus said to him, «Go your way; your faith has made you well.» And immediately he regained his sight and began following Him on the road.

Mark 11:22-24 ~ [22]And Jesus answered saying to them, «Have faith in God. [23]Truly I say to you, whoever says to this mountain, 'Be taken up and cast into the sea,' and does not doubt in his heart, but believes that what he says is going to happen, it shall be granted him. [24]Therefore I say to you, all things for which you pray and ask, believe that you have received them, and they shall be granted you."

Luke 8:43-48 ~ [43]And a woman who had a hemorrhage for twelve years, and could not be healed by anyone, [44]came up behind Him and touched the fringe of His cloak, and immediately her hemorrhage stopped. [45]And Jesus said, "Who is the one who touched Me?" And while they were all denying it, Peter said, "Master, the multitudes are crowding and pressing upon You." [46] But Jesus said, «Someone did touch Me, for I was aware that power had gone out of Me.» [47]And when the woman saw that she had not escaped notice, she came trembling and fell down before Him, and declared in the presence of all the people the reason why she had touched Him, and how she had been immediately healed. [48]And He said to her, «Daughter, your faith has made you well; go in peace.»

Luke 17:12-19 ~ [12]And as He entered a certain village, ten leprous men who stood at a distance met Him; [13]and they raised their voices, saying, «Jesus, Master, have mercy on us!» [14]And when He saw them, He said to them, «Go and show yourselves to the priests.» And it came about that as they were going, they were cleansed. [15]Now one of them, when he saw that he had been healed, turned back, glorifying God with a loud voice, [16]and he fell on his face at His feet, giving thanks to Him. And he was a Samaritan. [17]And Jesus answered and said, "Were there not ten cleansed? But the nine - where are they? [18]Was no one found who turned back to give glory to God, except this foreigner?" [19]And He said to him, «Rise and go your way; your faith has made you well.»

Luke 18:40-43 ~ [40]And Jesus stopped and commanded that he be brought to Him; and when he had come near, He questioned him, [41]»What do you want Me to do for you?» And he said, «Lord, I want to regain my sight!» [42]And Jesus said to him, «Receive your sight; your faith has made you well.» [43]And immediately he regained his sight, and began following Him, glorifying God; and when all the people saw it, they gave praise to God.

John 4:48-53 ~ [48]Jesus therefore said to him, «Unless you people see signs and wonders, you simply will not believe.» [49]The royal official said to Him, «Sir, come down before my child dies.» [50]Jesus said to him, «Go; your way; your son lives.» The man believed the word that Jesus spoke to him and he started off. [51]And as he was now going down, his slaves met him, saying that his son was living. [52]So he inquired of them the hour when he began to get better. They said therefore to him, «Yesterday at the seventh hour the fever left him.» [53]So the father knew that it was at that hour in which Jesus said to him, «Your son lives»; and he himself believed and his whole household.

Acts 3:16 ~ And on the basis of faith in His name, it is the name of Jesus which has strengthened this man whom you see and know; and the faith which comes through Him has given him this perfect health in the presence of you all.

Romans 4:19-21 ~ [19]And without becoming weak in faith he contemplated his own body, now as good as dead since he was about a hundred years old, and the deadness of Sarah's womb; [20]yet, with respect to the promise of God, he did not waver in unbelief, but grew strong in faith, giving glory to God, [21]and being fully assured that what He had promised, He was able also to perform.

Romans 10:17 ~ So faith comes from hearing, and hearing by the word of Christ.

2 Corinthians 4:13-14 ~ [13]But having the same spirit of faith, according to what is written, «I BELIEVED, THEREFORE I SPOKE,» we also believe, therefore also we speak; [14]Knowing that He who raised the Lord Jesus will raise us also with Jesus and will present us with you.

2 Corinthians 4:18 ~ While we look not at the things which are seen, but at the things which are not seen; for the things which are seen are temporal, but the things which are not seen are eternal.

2 Corinthians 5:7 ~ For we walk by faith, not by sight.

Galatians 3:5 ~ Does He then, who provides you with the Spirit and works miracles among you, do it by the works of the Law, or by hearing with faith?

Ephesians 6:16 ~ In addition to all, taking up the shield of faith with which you will be able to extinguish all the flaming missiles of the evil one.

1 Timothy 6:12 ~Fight the good fight of faith; take hold of the eternal life to which you were called and you made the good confession in the presence of many witnesses.

Hebrews 11:1-13, 17- 40 ~ [1]Now faith is the assurance of things hoped for, the conviction of things not seen. [2]For by it the men of old gained approval. [3]By faith we understand that the worlds were prepared by the word of God, so that what is seen was not made out of things which are visible. [4]By faith Abel offered to God a better sacrifice than Cain, through which he obtained the testimony that he was righteous, God testifying about his gifts, and through faith, though he is dead, he still speaks. [5]By faith Enoch was taken up so that he should not see death; AND HE WAS NOT FOUND BECAUSE GOD TOOK HIM UP; for he obtained the witness that before his being taken up he was pleasing to God. [6]And without faith it is impossible to please Him, for he who comes to God must believe that He is and that He is a rewarder of those who seek Him. [7]By faith Noah, being warned by God about things not yet seen, in reverence prepared an ark for the salvation of his household, by which he condemned the world, and became an heir of the righteousness which is according to faith. [8]By faith Abraham, when he was called, obeyed by going out to a place which he was to receive for an inheritance; and he went out, not knowing where he was going. [9]By faith he lived as an alien in the land of promise, as in a foreign land, dwelling in tents with Isaac and Jacob, fellow heirs of the same promise; [10]for he was looking for the city which has foundations, whose architect and builder is God. [11]By faith even Sarah herself received ability to conceive, even beyond the proper time of life, since she considered Him faithful who had promised; [12]therefore, also, there was born of one man, and him as good as dead at that, as many descendants AS THE STARS OF HEAVEN IN NUMBER, AND INNUMERABLE AS THE SAND WHICH IS BY THE SEASHORE. [13]All theses died in faith, without receiving the promises, but having seen them and having confessed that they were strangers and exiles on the earth... [17]By faith Abraham, when he was tested, offered up Isaac; and he who had received the promises was offering up his only begotten son; [18]it was he to whom it was said, IN ISAAC YOUR DESCENDANTS SHALL BE CALLED." [19]He considered that God is able to raise men even from the dead; from which he also received him back as a type. [20]By faith Isaac blessed Jacob and Esau, even regarding things to come. [21]By faith Jacob, as he was dying, blessed each of the sons of Joseph, and worshiped, leaning on the top of his staff. [22]By faith Joseph, when he was dying, made mention of the exodus of the sons of Israel, and gave orders concerning his bones. [23]By faith Moses, when he was born, was hidden for three months by his parents, because they saw he was a beautiful child; and they were not afraid of the king's edict. [24]By faith Moses, when he had grown up, refused to be called the son of Pharaoh's daughter; [25]choosing rather to endure ill-treatment with the people of God, than to enjoy the passing pleasures of sin; [26]considering the reproach of Christ greater riches than the treasures of Egypt; for he was looking to the reward. [27]By faith he left Egypt, not fearing the wrath of the king; for he endured, as seeing Him who is unseen. [28]By faith he kept the Passover and the sprinkling of blood, so that he who destroyed the first-born might not touch them. [29]By faith they passed through the Red Sea as though they were passing through dry land; and the Egyptians, when they attempted it, were drowned. [30]By faith the walls of Jericho fell down, after they had been encircled for seven days. [31]By faith Rahab the harlot did not perish along with those who were disobedient, after she had welcomed the spies in peace. [32]And what more shall I say? For time will fail me is I tell Gideon, Barak, Samson, Jephthah, of David and Samuel and the prophets, [33]who by faith conquered kingdoms, performed acts of righteousness, obtained promises, shut the mouths of lions, [34]quenched the power of fire, escaped the edge of the sword, from weakness were made strong, became mighty in war, put foreign armies to flight. [35]Women received back their dead by resurrection; and others were tortured, not accepting their release, in order that they might obtain a better resurrection; [36]and others experienced mockings and scourgings, yes, also chains and imprisonment. [37]They were stoned, they were sawn in two, they were tempted, they were put to death with the sword; they went about in sheepskins, in goatskins, being destitute, afflicted, ill-treated [38](men of whom the world was not worthy), wandering in deserts and mountains and caves and holes in the ground. [39]And all these, having gained approval through their faith, did not receive what was promised, [40]because God had provided something better for us, so that apart from us they should not be made perfect.

James 1:6-8 ~ [6]But let him ask in faith without any doubting, for the one who doubts is like the surf of the sea driven and tossed by the wind. [7]For let not that man expect that he will receive anything from the Lord, [8]being a double-minded man, unstable in all his ways.

1 John 3:21-22 ~ [21]Beloved, if our heart does not condemn us, we have confidence before God; [22]and whatever we ask we receive from Him, because we keep His commandments and do the things that are pleasing in His sight.

1 John 5:4-5 ~ [4]For whatever is born of God overcomes the world; and this is the victory that has overcome the world - our faith. [5]And who is the one who overcomes the world, but he who believes that Jesus is the Son of God?

1 John 5:14-15 ~ [14]And this is the confidence which we have before Him, that, if we ask anything according to His will, He hears us. [15]And if we know that He hears us in whatever we ask, we know that He hears us in whatever we ask, we know that we have the requests which we have asked from Him.

This chapter is a journey through the scriptures, tracing the footprints of faith from the Gospels to the Epistles, offering us profound insights into the strength, resilience, and transformative power of faith. We've seen how faith fueled miraculous healings, moved mountains, and manifested the impossible.

The Book of Hebrews gives us the quintessential definition of faith - «the assurance of things hoped for, the conviction of things not seen.» It provides a roll-call of the heroes of faith - from Abel to Enoch, from Noah to Abraham and Sarah - all who, by their belief in God's promises, became conduits of His divine power.

The scriptures reveal that faith is not merely a passive acceptance, but a dynamic force that actively shapes our relationship with God. They demonstrate that it is through faith we perceive the eternal within the temporal, see the invisible within the visible, and experience the infinite within the finite.

As we continue our spiritual journey, let us remember these stories of faith - stories that inspire us, challenge us, and urge us to carry our own shield of faith. For it is faith that brings healing and hope, that overcomes the world and pleases God. It empowers us to look beyond what is seen, to anticipate God's promises, and to live as children of the Kingdom.

As we move to the next chapter, may we carry with us the light of faith that illuminates even the darkest corners and the power of belief that makes the impossible, possible.

The Miraculous

As we open the chapter, "The Miraculous," we delve deep into the potent essence of faith, a beacon that illuminates the boundless power of belief in the divine, the Son of God, Jesus Christ. We are embarking on a journey through the life-altering narratives from the sacred scriptures, each a testament to the astounding miracles enabled by faith.

Faith, in its deepest and purest form, is the path that brings us closer to God's glory. In the profound words of Jesus from the Gospel of Mark, "Do not be afraid any longer, only believe," we see the cornerstone of our faith. Jesus, in His infinite compassion and boundless love, restores health, revives life, and above all, ignites the flame of faith in those who seek Him.

The scriptures unfold a panorama of miracles, each more awe-inspiring than the last. From the man with the withered hand restored to full health to the awakening of the young girl from her deathlike slumber, from the paralytic man regaining his strength to the resurrection of Lazarus from the tomb, we witness the Divine at work. These were not merely acts of physical healing; they were manifestations of spiritual renewal, an awakening brought forth through unwavering faith in Jesus.

Through the eyes of Peter and John, we observe the miraculous power of faith extend beyond the time of

Jesus. The lame man, strengthened by faith, walks in the glory of God; Tabitha, once dead, now alive, serves as a symbol of renewed hope and belief; Aeneas, paralyzed for years, is freed from his bed; and Eutychus, thought dead, is revived and serves as an undeniable testament of faith.

As we explore these miracles, may the truths of these scriptures inspire and strengthen your faith, helping you to see beyond the visible, reaching towards the realm of the miraculous, that is found in our Lord Jesus Christ.

Mark 3:3-5 ~ [3]And He said to the man with the withered hand, «Rise and come forward!» [4]And He said to them, «Is it lawful on the Sabbath to do good or to do harm, to save a life or to kill?» But they kept silent. [5]And after looking around at them with anger, grieved at their hardness of heart, He said to the man, «Stretch out your hand.» And he stretched it out, and his hand was restored.

Mark 5:35-36,38-42 ~ [35]»While He was still speaking, they came from the house of the synagogue official, saying, "Your daughter has died; why trouble the Teacher anymore?» [36]But Jesus, overhearing what was being spoken, said to the synagogue official, "Do not be afraid any longer, only believe."... [38]And they came to the house of the synagogue official; and He

41

beheld a commotion, and people loudly weeping and wailing. [39]And entering in, He said to them, "Why make a commotion and weep? The child has not died, but is asleep." [40]And they began laughing at Him. But putting them all out, He took along the child's father and mother and His own companions, and entered the room where the child was. [41]And taking the child by the hand, He said to her, «Talitha kum!» (which translated means, «Little girl, I say to you, arise!»). 42And immediately the girl rose and began to walk; for she was twelve years old. And immediately they were completely astounded.

Luke 5:17-20, 24-26 ~ [17]And it came about one day that He was teaching; and there were some Pharisees and teachers of the law sitting there, who had come from every village of Galilee and Judea and from Jerusalem; and the power of the Lord was present for Him to perform healing. [18]And behold, some men were carrying on a bed a man who was paralyzed; and they were trying to bring him in, and to set him down in front of Him. [19]And not finding any way to bring him in because of the crowd, they went up on the roof and let him down through the tiles with his stretcher, right in the centre, in front of Jesus. [20]And seeing their faith, He said, «Friend, your sins are forgiven you.».…[24]»But in order that you may know that the Son of Man has authority on earth to forgive sins,» - He said to the paralytic - »I say to you, rise, and take up your stretcher and go home.» [25]And at once he rose up before them, and took up what he had been lying on, and went home, glorifying God. [26]And they were all seized with astonishment and began glorifying God; and they were filled with fear, saying, «We have seen remarkable things today.»

Luke 7:12-16 ~ [12]Now as He approached the gate of the city, behold, a dead man was being carried out, the only son of his mother, and she was a widow; and a sizeable crowd from the city was with her. [13]And when the Lord saw her, He felt compassion for her, and said to her, «Do not weep.» [14]And He came up and touched the coffin; and the bearers came to a halt. And He said, «Young man, I say to you, arise!» [15]And the dead man sat up and began to speak. And Jesus gave him back to his mother. [16]And fear gripped them all, and they began glorifying God, saying, "A great prophet has arisen among us!" and, "God has visited His people!"

John 11:1-4, 11-15, 17, 21-27, 39-45 ~ [1]Now a certain man was sick, Lazarus of Bethany, the village of Mary and her sister Martha. [2]And it was the Mary who anointed the Lord with ointment, and wiped His feet with her hair, whose brother Lazarus was sick. [3]The sisters therefore sent to Him, saying, «Lord, behold, he whom You love is sick.» [4]But when Jesus heard it, He said, «This sickness is not unto death, but for the glory of God, that the Son of God may be glorified by it.»... [11]This He said, and after

43

that He said to them, «Our friend Lazarus has fallen asleep; but I go, that I may awaken him out of sleep.» [12]The disciples therefore said to Him, «Lord, if he has fallen asleep, he will recover.» [13]Now Jesus had spoken of his death, but they thought that He was speaking of literal sleep. [14]Then Jesus therefore said to them plainly, «Lazarus is dead,[15]and I am glad for your sakes that I was not there, so that you may believe; but let us go to him.».... [17]So when Jesus came, He found that he had already been in the tomb four days.... [21]Martha therefore said to Jesus, «Lord, if You had been here, my brother would not have died. [22]»Even now I know that whatever You ask of God, God will give You.» [23]Jesus said to her, «Your brother shall rise again.» [24]Martha said to Him, "I know that he will rise again in the resurrection on the last day." [25]Jesus said to her, «I am the resurrection and the life; he who believes in Me shall live even if he dies, [26]and everyone who lives and believes in Me shall never die. Do you believe this?» [27]She said to Him, «Yes, Lord; I have believed that You are the Christ, the Son of God, even He who comes into the world.».... [39]Jesus said, «Remove the stone.» Martha, the sister of the deceased, said to Him, «Lord, by this time there will be a stench, for he has been dead four days.» [40]Jesus said to her, «Did I not say to you, if you believe, you will see the glory of God?» [41]And so they removed the stone. And Jesus raised His eyes, and said, «Father, I thank Thee that Thou heardest Me. [42]»And I knew that Thou hearest Me always; but because of the people standing around I said it, so that they may believe that Thou didst send Me.» [43]And when He had said these things, He cried out with a loud voice, «Lazarus, come forth.» [44]He who had died came forth, bound hand and foot with wrappings, and his face was wrapped around with a cloth. Jesus said to them, «Unbind him, and let him go.» [45]Many therefore of the Jews, who had come to Mary and beheld what He had done, believed in Him.

Acts 3:1-9 ~ [1]Now Peter and John were going up to the temple at the ninth hour, the hour of prayer. [2]And a certain man who had been lame from his mother's womb was being carried along, whom they used to set down every day at the gate of the temple which is called Beautiful, in order to beg alms of those who were entering the temple. [3]And when he saw Peter and John about to go into the temple, he began asking to receive alms. [4]And Peter, along with John, fixed his gaze upon him and said, "Look at us!" [5]And he began to give them his attention, expecting to receive something from them. [6]But Peter said, «I do not possess silver and gold, but what I do have I give to you: In the name of Jesus Christ the Nazarene--walk!» [7]And seizing him by the right hand, he raised him up; and immediately his feet and his ankles were strengthened. [8]And with a leap, he stood upright and began to walk; and he entered the temple with them, walking and leaping and praising God. [9]And all the people saw him walking and praising God.

Acts 9:36-42 ~ ³⁶Now in Joppa there was a certain disciple named Tabitha (which translated in Greek is called Dorcas); this woman was abounding with deeds of kindness and charity, which she continually did. ³⁷And it came about at that time that she fell sick and died; and when they had washed her body, they laid it in an upper room. ³⁸And since Lydda was near Joppa, the disciples, having heard that Peter was there, sent two men to him, entreating him, "Do not delay to come to us." ³⁹And Peter arose and went with them. And when he had come, they brought him into the upper room; and all the windows stood beside him weeping, and showing all the tunics and garments that Dorcas used to make while she was with them. ⁴⁰But Peter sent them all out and knelt down and prayed, and turning to the body, he said, «Tabitha, arise.» And she opened her eyes, and when she saw Peter, she sat up. ⁴¹And he gave her his hand and raised her up; and calling the saints and widows, he presented her alive. ⁴²And it became known all over Joppa, and many believed in the Lord.

Acts 9:32-35 ~ ³²Now it came about that as Peter was traveling through all those parts, he came down also to the saints who lived at Lydda. ³³And there he found a certain man named Aeneas, who had been bedridden eight years, for he was paralyzed. ³⁴And Peter said to him, «Aeneas, Jesus Christ heals you; arise and make your bed.» And immediately he arose. [35]And all who lived at Lydda and Sharon saw him, and they turned to the Lord.

Acts 20:9-10, 12 ~ [9]And there was a certain young man named Eutychus sitting on the window sill, sinking into a deep sleep; and as Paul kept on talking, he was overcome by sleep and fell down from the third floor, and was picked up dead. [10]But Paul went down and fell upon him and after embracing him, he said, «Do not be troubled, for his life is in him.»... [12]And they took away the boy alive, and were greatly comforted.

As we draw this chapter to a close, let us reflect upon the extraordinary journey we have traversed. The narratives of faith, the miracles, and the life-altering transformations are not mere stories from an ancient past; they serve as profound lessons and inspirations for us in our own spiritual journey.

Each miracle, whether it was the restoration of the withered hand, the awakening of the young girl, the healing of the paralytic man, or the resurrection of Lazarus, is a beacon of hope. It teaches us that faith in the divine, in the compassionate and loving Jesus Christ, can bring forth miracles, irrespective of the circumstances.

Moreover, the miracles performed by Peter and John remind us that faith, illuminated by love and devotion to

Christ, can manifest divine power and deliver miracles. The stories of the lame man walking, Tabitha returning to life, Aeneas rising from his bed, and Eutychus regaining his life, speak volumes about the ceaseless power of faith.

These scriptures offer us a comforting embrace, gently reassuring us that faith in Christ, the Son of God, is our pathway to experiencing the miraculous in our lives. It is a testament to the timeless wisdom that faith can indeed move mountains, heal the deepest of wounds, and even breathe life where there was none.

As you close this chapter, let the essence of these stories linger in your heart, inspiring you to nurture and cultivate your faith. For in faith, there is hope; in faith, there is healing; and in faith, there is life everlasting. Remember, even in moments of darkness and despair, the light of faith can guide us toward the miraculous, toward the glory of God, toward our Lord and Saviour, Jesus Christ.

Healing and Deliverance

As we journey together through this sacred chapter on Healing and Deliverance, let us find solace in the compassionate healing narratives shared throughout the New Testament. Grounded firmly in the Gospel, these scriptures reaffirm the profound healing ministry of Jesus Christ, our compassionate Redeemer, and the enduring faith that lies at the heart of the Christian life.

We find ourselves immersed in the narratives of Matthew, Mark, Luke, and Acts, where Jesus reached out to the sick, the bereaved, and the marginalized, touching their lives with transformative power. Through His grace, the feverish are cooled, the lame walk, the blind see, the lepers are cleansed, and the dead are brought back to life. His words are not merely comforting metaphors; they are the testament of divine truth, demonstrating the power of faith, love, and the Holy Spirit.

In each scripture, healing is not merely a physical act, but a spiritual deliverance, a liberation from suffering, and a powerful manifestation of God's boundless mercy. These healing narratives are not confined to ancient times, they continue to resonate in our lives today, affirming that God's compassion, love, and mercy are ceaselessly active in our world.

We are reminded through Paul's teachings in 2 Corinthians and Galatians that where the Spirit of the Lord is, there is liberty. It is in Christ that we find true freedom, and it is through His love that we are unshackled from the burdens of pain, illness, and sin.

May this chapter inspire faith and resilience in our hearts, providing comfort to those in need and fostering a deep-seated assurance of Christ's healing love in every phase of our lives.

Matthew 8:14-15 ~ [14]And when Jesus had come to Peter's home, He saw his mother-in-law lying sick in bed with a fever. [15]And He touched her hand, and the fever left her; and she arose, and waited on Him.

Matthew 9:18b-19, 24-25 ~ [18]...Behold there came a synagogue official, and bowed down before Him, saying, "My daughter has just died; but come and lay your hand on her, and she will live. [19]And Jesus rose and began to follow him, and so did His disciples...[24]He began to say, «Depart; for the girl has not died, but is asleep.» And they began laughing at Him. [25]But when the crowd had been put out, He entered and took her by the hand; and the girl arose.

Matthew 12:15 ~ But Jesus, aware of this, withdrew from there. And many followed Him, and He healed them all.

Matthew 14:14 ~ And when He went ashore, He saw a great multitude, and felt compassion for them, and healed their sick.

Matthew 19:1-2 ~ [1]And it came about that when Jesus had finished these words, He departed from Galilee, and came into the region of Judea beyond the Jordan; [2]and great multitudes followed Him, and He healed them there.

Matthew 20:34 ~ And moved with compassion, Jesus touched their eyes; and immediately they regained their sight and followed Him.

Matthew 21:14 ~ And the blind and the lame came to Him in the temple, and He healed them.

Mark 1:40-42 ~ [40]And a leper came to Him, beseeching Him and falling on his knees before Him, and saying to Him, «If You are willing, You can make me clean.» [41]And moved with compassion, He stretched out His hand, and touched him, and said to him, «I am willing; be cleansed.» [42]And immediately the leprosy left him and he was cleansed.

Mark 6:13 ~ And they were casting out many demons and were anointing with oil many sick people and healing them.

Mark 6:56 ~ And wherever He entered villages, or cities, or countryside, they were laying the sick in the market places, and entreating Him that they might just touch the fringe of His cloak; and as many as touched it were being cured.

Mark 7:32-35,37 ~ [32]And they brought to Him one who was deaf and spoke with difficulty, and they entreated Him to lay His hand upon him. [33]And He took him aside from the multitude by himself, and put His fingers into his ears, and after spitting, He touched his tongue with the saliva; [34]and looking up to heaven with a deep sigh, He said to him, «Ephphatha!» that is, «Be opened!» [35]And his ears were opened, and the impediment of his tongue was removed, and he began speaking plainly....[37]And they were utterly astonished, saying, «He has done all things well; He makes even the deaf to hear, and the dumb to speak.»

Luke 6:6, 9-10 ~ [6]And it came about on another Sabbath, that He entered the synagogue and was teaching; and there was a man there whose right hand was withered...[9]And Jesus said to them, «I ask you, is it lawful on the Sabbath to do good, or to do harm, to save a life, or to destroy it?» ¹⁰And after looking around at them all, He said to him, «Stretch out your hand!» And he did so; and his hand was restored.

Luke 6:17-19 ~ ¹⁷And He descended with them, and stood on a level place; and there was a great multitude of His disciples, and a great throng of people from all Judea and Jerusalem and the coastal region of Tyre and Sidon, ¹⁸who had come to hear Him, and to be healed of their diseases; and those who were troubled with unclean spirits were being cured. ¹⁹And all the multitude were trying to touch Him, for power was coming from Him and healing them all.

Luke 7:2-10 ~ ²And a certain centurion's slave, who was highly regarded by him, was sick and about to die. ³And when he heard about Jesus, he sent some Jewish elders asking Him to come and save the life of his slave. ⁴And when they had come to Jesus, they earnestly entreated Him, saying, "He is worthy for You to grant this to him; ⁵for he loves our nation, and it was he who built us our synagogue." ⁶Now Jesus started on His way with them; and when He was already not far from the house, the centurion sent friends, saying to Him, "Lord, do not trouble Yourself further, for I am not worthy for You to come under my roof; ⁷for this reason I did not even consider myself worthy to come to You, but just say the word, and my servant will be healed. [8]For I, too, am a man under authority, with soldiers under me; and I say to this one, 'Go!' and he goes; and to another, 'Come!' and he comes; and to my slave, 'Do this!' and he does it.» [9]Now when Jesus heard this, He marvelled at him, and turned and said to the multitude that was following Him, «I say to you, not even in Israel have I found such great faith.» [10]And when those who had been sent returned to the house, they found the slave in good health.

Luke 7:21-22 ~ [21]At that very time He cured many people of diseases and afflictions and evil spirits; and He granted sight to many who were blind. [22]And He answered and said to them, «Go and report to John what you have seen and heard: the BLIND RECEIVE SIGHT, the lame walk, the lepers are cleansed, and the deaf hear, the dead are raised up, the POOR HAVE THE GOSPEL PREACHED TO THEM."

Luke 8:49-55 ~ [49]While He was still speaking, someone came from the house of the synagogue official, saying, "Your daughter has died; do not trouble the Teacher anymore." [50]But when Jesus heard this, He answered him, «Do not be afraid any longer; only believe, and she shall be made well.» [51]And when He had come to the house, He did not allow anyone to enter with Him, except Peter and John and James, and the girl's father and mother. [52]Now they were all weeping and lamenting for her; but He said, «Stop weeping, for she has not died, but is asleep.» [53]And they began laughing at Him, knowing that she had died. [54]He, however, took her by the hand and called, saying, «Child, arise!» [55]And her spirit returned, and she rose immediately; and He gave orders for something to be given her to eat.

Luke 9:11 ~ But the multitudes were aware of this and followed Him; and welcoming them, He began speaking to them about the kingdom of God and curing those who had need of healing.

Luke 10:8-9 ~ [8]"And whatever city you enter, and they receive you, eat what is set before you; [9]and heal those in it who are sick, and say to them, 'The kingdom of God has come near to you.'"

Luke 13:11-13 ~ [11]And behold, there was a woman who for eighteen years had had a sickness caused by a spirit; and she was bent double, and could not straighten up at all. [12]And when Jesus saw her, He called her over and said to her, «Woman, you are freed from your sickness.» [13]And He laid His hands upon her; and immediately she was made erect again, and began glorifying God.

Luke 14:2-4 ~ [2]And there, in front of Him was a certain man suffering from dropsy. [3]And Jesus answered and spoke to the lawyers and Pharisees, saying, «Is it lawful to heal on the Sabbath, or not?» [4]But they kept silent. And He took hold of him and healed him, and sent him away.

Luke 22:50-51 ~ [50]And a certain one of them struck the slave of the high priest and cut off his right ear. [51]But Jesus answered and said, «Stop! No more of this.» And He touched his ear and healed him.

Acts 14:8-10 ~ [8]And at Lystra there was sitting a certain man, without strength in his feet, lame from his mother's womb, who had never walked. [9]This man was listening to Paul as he spoke, who, when he had fixed his gaze upon him and had seen that he had faith to be made well, [10]said with a loud voice, «Stand upright on your feet.» And he leaped up and began to walk.

Acts 28:8-9 ~ [8]And it happened that the father of Publius was lying in bed afflicted with recurrent fever and dysentery; and Paul went in to see him and after he had prayed, he laid his hands on him and healed him. [9]And after this had happened, the rest of the people on the island who had diseases were coming to him and getting cured.

2 Corinthians 3:17 ~ [17]Now the Lord is the Spirit; and where the Spirit of the Lord is, there is liberty.

Galatians 5:1 ~ [1]It was for freedom that Christ set us free; therefore keep standing firm and do not be subject again to a yoke of slavery.

James 5:14-16 ~ [14]Is anyone among you sick? Let him call for the elders of the church, and let them pray over him, anointing him with oil in the name of the Lord; [15]and the prayer offered in faith will restore the one who is sick, and the Lord will raise him up, and if he has committed sins, they will be forgiven him. [16]Therefore, confess your sins to one another, and pray for one another, so that you may be healed. The effective prayer of a righteous man can accomplish much.

This chapter on Healing and Deliverance draws to a close, leaving us inspired and hopeful. From the depths of our hearts, may we embody the teachings of the scriptures, nurturing our faith in Christ's healing power, and extending that same compassion and love towards others.

The Gospel's narratives show us that the call to healing extends beyond the self. As seen in James' epistle, we are reminded to reach out to others in prayer, anointing the sick in the name of the Lord. In these acts of faith, there is a promise of restoration and forgiveness of sins, encapsulating the theme of healing and deliverance.

The effective prayer of the righteous is potent and can bring about much change, as James affirms. Prayer, then, becomes our intimate dialogue with God, a means of laying bare our vulnerabilities, hopes, and needs before His benevolent gaze. It is an act of faith that trusts in God's power to mend, restore, and make whole.

In closing, we rest in the assurance that God's power to heal remains undiminished. Through Christ, we have glimpsed the reality of this healing power. We move forward knowing that His compassion is as alive today as it was in the time of the Gospels. As we experience suffering or confront afflictions, let us always turn to Christ, the Healer, in unwavering faith.

May this chapter serve as a reminder of the enduring promise of God's healing grace and the liberating power of Christ's love, providing comfort, strength, and hope to all who seek it. Amen.

Signs and Wonders

In the sacred whisper of the scriptures, we encounter an undeniable testament of the boundless love and grace of our Lord, Jesus Christ. The chapter that lies before you, «Signs and Wonders,» is a divine tapestry woven with the threads of faith and miracles, of compassion and healing. It plunges into the narratives of our Savior's ministry, his works that moved mountains, and the unfathomable depths of his mercy, as chronicled in the Gospel.

The verses recounted in this chapter, lifted from the divine pages of Matthew, Mark, Luke, John, and the Acts of the Apostles, bear witness to the miraculous power and authority of Jesus Christ. They narrate the radiant instances where our Lord, with a mere touch or word, healed the sick, forgave sins, gave sight to the blind, speech to the mute, and mobility to the lame. They testify to the instances where the simple faith of the afflicted and their loved ones elicited from Jesus, healing and liberation beyond their wildest expectations.

As you delve into these scriptures, reflect upon the authority bestowed upon the disciples to cast out unclean spirits and to heal every kind of disease and sickness, echoing the power and love of Christ. Ponder the awe and glorification of God that reverberated among the multitudes when they witnessed the signs and wonders performed by our Lord.

In reading these verses, we pray that your heart may be open to the transformative power of faith and that your spirit may be uplifted by the love of our Lord. As the mountains of affliction crumble, may the wonders of His love be the signs that guide you along your spiritual journey.

Matthew 4:23-24 ~ [23] And Jesus was going about in all Galilee, teaching in their synagogues, and proclaiming the gospel of the kingdom, and healing every kind of disease and every kind of sickness among the people. [24] And the news about Him went out into all Syria; and they brought to Him all who were ill, taken with various diseases and pains, demoniacs, epileptics, paralytics; and He healed them.

Matthew 9:2, 6-8 ~ [2] And behold, they were bringing to Him a paralytic, lying on a bed; and Jesus seeing their faith, said to the paralytic, «Take courage, My son, your sins are forgiven.»...[6] »But in order that you may know that the Son of Man has authority on earth to forgive sins» - then He said to the paralytic - «Rise, take up your bed, and go home.» [7] And he rose, and went home. 8But when the multitudes saw this, they were filled with awe, and glorified God, who had given such authority to men.

Matthew 9:32-33 ~ [32]And as they were going out, behold, a dumb man, demon-possessed, was brought to Him. [33]And after the demon was cast out, the dumb man spoke; and the multitudes marveled, saying, «Nothing like this was ever seen in Israel.»

Matthew 9:35 ~ And Jesus was going about all the cities and the villages, teaching in their synagogues, and proclaiming the gospel of the kingdom, and healing every kind of disease and every kind of sickness.

Matthew 10:1 ~ And having summoned His twelve disciples, He gave them authority over unclean spirits, to cast them out, and to heal every kind of disease and every kind of sickness.

Matthew 10:7-8 ~ [7]"And as you go, preach, saying, 'The kingdom of heaven is at hand.' [8]»Heal the sick, raise the dead, cleanse the lepers, cast out demons; freely you received, freely give."

Matthew 11:4-5 ~ [4]And Jesus answered and said to them, "Go and report to John what you hear and see: 5the BLIND RECEIVE SIGHT and the lame walk, the lepers are cleansed and the deaf hear, the dead are raised up, and the POOR HAVE THE GOSPEL PREACHED TO THEM."

Matthew 12:10-13 ~ [10]And behold, there was a man with a withered hand. And they questioned Him, saying, "Is it lawful to heal on the Sabbath?" - in order that they might accuse Him. [11]And He said to them, «What man shall there be among you, who shall have one sheep, and if it falls into a pit on the Sabbath, will he not take hold of it and lift it out? [12]»Of how much more value then is a man than a sheep! So then, it is lawful to do good on the Sabbath.» [13]Then He said to the man, «Stretch out your hand!» And he stretched it out, and it was restored to normal, like the other.

Matthew 15:30-31 ~ [30]And great multitudes came to Him, bringing with them those who were lame, crippled, blind, dumb, and many others, and they laid them down at His feet; and He healed them, [31]so that the multitude marvelled as they saw the dumb speaking, the crippled restored, and the lame walking, and the blind seeing; and they glorified the God of Israel.

Mark 2:3-5,10-12 ~ [3]And they came, bringing to Him a paralytic, carried by four men. [4]And being unable to get to Him because of the crowd, they removed the roof above Him; and when they had dug an opening, they let down the pallet on which the paralytic was lying. [5]And Jesus seeing their faith said to the paralytic, «My son, your sins are forgiven.».... [10]"But in order that you may know that the Son of Man has authority on earth to forgive sins" - He said to the paralytic - [11]"I say to you, rise, take up your pallet and go home." [12]And he rose and immediately took up the pallet and went out in the sight of all; so that they were all amazed and were glorifying God, saying, «We have never seen anything like this.»

Mark 16:17-18 ~ [17]»And these signs will accompany those who have believed: in My name they will cast out demons, they will speak with new tongues; [18]they will pick up serpents, and if they drink any deadly poison, it shall not hurt them: they will lay hands on the sick, and they will recover.»

Mark 16:20 ~ And they went out and preached everywhere, while the Lord worked with them, and confirmed the word by the signs that followed.

Luke 4:18-19 ~ [18] «The Spirit of the Lord is upon me, because He anointed me to preach the gospel to the poor. He has sent me to proclaim release to the captives, and recovery of sight to the blind, to set free those who are down-trodden, 1^9 to proclaim the favorable year of the Lord.»

Luke 5:12-13,15 ~ ^{12}And it came about that while He was in one of the cities, behold, there was a man full leprosy; and when he saw Jesus, he fell on his face and implored Him, saying, «Lord, if You are willing, You can make me clean.» ^{13}And He stretched out His hand, and touched him, saying, «I am willing; be cleansed.» And immediately the leprosy left him... ^{15}But the news about Him was spreading even farther, and great multitudes were gathering to hear Him and to be healed of their sicknesses.

Luke 8:1-2 ~ ^{1}And it came about soon after wards, that He began going about from one city and village to another, proclaiming and preaching the kingdom of God; and the twelve were with Him, ^{2}and also some women who had been healed of evil spirits and sicknesses: Mary who was called Magdalene, from whom seven demons had gone out.

Luke 9:1-2, 6 ~ ^{1}And He called the twelve together, and gave them power and authority over all the demons, and to heal diseases. ^{2}And He sent them out to proclaim the kingdom of God, and to perform healing... 6And departing, they began going about among the villages, preaching the gospel, and healing everywhere.

John 2:23 ~ Now when He was in Jerusalem at the Passover, during the feast, many believed in His name, beholding His signs which He was doing.

John 3:2 ~ this man came to Him by night, and said to Him, «Rabbi, we know that You have come from God as a teacher; for no one can do these signs that You do unless God is with him.»

John 6:2 ~ And a great multitude was following Him, because they were seeing the signs which He was performing on those who were sick.

John 9:1-3, 6-7 ~ ¹And as He passed by, He saw a man blind from birth. ²And His disciples asked Him, saying, «Rabbi, who sinned, this man or his parents, that he should be born blind?» ³Jesus answered, «It was neither that this man sinned, nor his parents; but it was in order that the works of God might be displayed in him...» ⁶When He had said this, He spat on the ground, and made clay of the spittle, and applied the clay to his eyes, ⁷and said to him, «Go, wash in the pool of Siloam» (which is translated, Sent). And so he went away and washed, and came back seeing.

John 12:17-18 ~ [17]And so the multitude who were with Him when He called Lazarus out of the tomb, and raised him from the dead, were bearing Him witness. [18]For this cause also the multitude went and met Him, because they heard that He had performed this sign.

John 20:30-31 ~ [30]Therefore many other signs Jesus also performed in the presence of the disciples, which are not written in this book; [31]but these have been written so that you may believe that Jesus is the Christ, the Son of God; and that believing you may have life in His name.

Acts 2:43 ~ And everyone kept feeling a sense of awe; and many wonders and signs were taking place through the apostles.

Acts 5:12, 15-16 ~ And at the hands of the apostles many signs and wonders were taking place among the people; and they were all with one accord in Solomon's portico...[15]to such an extent that they even carried the sick out into the streets and laid them on cots and pallets, so that when Peter came by, at least his shadow might fall on any one of them. [16]And also the people from the cities in the vicinity of Jerusalem were coming together, bringing people who were sick or afflicted with unclean spirits, and they were all being healed.

Acts 6:8 ~ And Stephen, full of grace and power, was performing great wonders and signs among the people.

Acts 8:6-7 ~ [6]And the multitudes with one accord were giving attention to what was said by Philip, as they heard and saw the signs which he was performing. [7]For in the case of many who had unclean spirits, they were coming out of them shouting with a loud voice; and many who had been paralyzed and lame were healed.

Acts 8:13 ~ And even Simon himself believed; and after being baptized, he continued on with Philip, and as he observed signs and great miracles taking place, he was constantly amazed.

Acts 14:3 ~ Therefore they spent a long time there speaking boldly with reliance upon the Lord, who was bearing witness to the word of His grace, granting that signs and wonders be done by their hands.

Acts 19:11-12 ~ [11]And God was performing extraordinary miracles by the hands of Paul, [12]so that handkerchiefs or aprons were even carried from his body to the sick, and the diseases left them and the evil spirits went out.

Romans 15:18-19 ~ [18]For I will not presume to speak of anything except what Christ has accomplished through me, resulting in the obedience of the Gentiles by word and deed, [19]in the power of signs and wonders, in the power of the Spirit; so that from Jerusalem and round about as far as Illyricum I have fully preached the gospel of Christ.

2 Corinthians 12:12 ~ The signs of a true apostle were performed among you with all perseverance, by signs and wonders and miracles.

Having journeyed through the «Signs and Wonders» of our Lord Jesus Christ, we emerge with hearts aglow and spirits lifted. The chapter bore testament to the compassionate heart of our Savior, His unfailing love, and His undeniable authority. His miracles, extending beyond physical healing, were signs of the divine kingdom, igniting hope, strengthening faith, and revealing God's glory.

These narratives serve as a reminder that our Lord sees beyond our physical ailments, reaching into the depths of our souls, addressing the spiritual maladies that bind us, and setting us free. His miraculous acts were not merely demonstrations of divine power but were expressions of divine love. Each healing, each act of forgiveness, was a restoration, a homecoming of a soul to its heavenly Father.

As we part from this chapter, let us carry forward the lessons of faith and perseverance. Let these stories of signs and wonders inspire us to approach our Savior with the faith of the paralytic and his friends, the humility of the man with leprosy, and the persistence of the many who simply believed in His healing touch.

In the grand tapestry of our lives, let these scriptures serve as golden threads, reminding us of God's unfailing love and the promise of healing and salvation in Jesus Christ. May the signs and wonders performed by our Lord not remain as ancient stories, but come alive in our daily walks of faith, encouraging us, inspiring us, and drawing us closer to His heart. May we echo the disciples and apostles, bringing about spiritual healing and demonstrating the kingdom of God in our world today. For in the signs and wonders of Christ, we find hope, and in His love, we find life.

Authority over Unclean Spirits and Demons

In the quietude of our hearts and the tranquility of our souls, we find ourselves at the foot of an unseen mountain — a looming, unspoken presence that pervades our lives with shadows. These are the mountains of our doubts, our fears, and sometimes, the unclean spirits and demons that may try to gain control of our lives. As we embark on this journey through the pages of this chapter, «Authority over Unclean Spirits and Demons,» we delve into the transformative teachings of Christ, who showed us through his actions and parables that the power of faith and the authority of God's love can cast out even the deepest-seated unclean spirits.

In the Gospel of Matthew, we witness Jesus' authority over unclean spirits, his steadfast faith and the powerful reassurance that, «if you have faith as a mustard seed, you shall say to this mountain, 'Move from here to there,' and it shall move; and nothing shall be impossible to you.» As we explore the various instances in which Jesus encounters and expels unclean spirits and demons, we will seek to understand how His teachings guide us to assert our own spiritual authority, reinforce our faith, and move the mountains in our own lives.

Together, let us journey through the scriptures, unearthing the deep-seated truths that reside in the accounts of Mark, Luke, and Matthew. Let us bravely face the mountains before us, armed with the Word of God, and embrace the limitless power of faith and the authority bestowed upon us by His love.

Matthew 12:22 ~ Then there was brought to Him a demon-possessed man who was blind and dumb, and He healed him, so that the dumb man spoke and saw.

Matthew 12:28 ~ «But if I cast out demons by the Spirit of God, then the kingdom of God has come upon you."

Matthew 17:15-20 ~ [15]"Lord, have mercy on my son, for he is a lunatic, and is very ill; for he often falls into the fire, and often into the water. [16]"And I brought him to Your disciples, and they could not cure him." [17]And Jesus answered and said, «O unbelieving and perverted generation, how long shall I be with you? How long shall I put up with you? Bring him here to Me.» [18]And Jesus rebuked him, and the demon came out of him, and the boy was cured at once. [19]Then the disciples came to Jesus privately and said, "Why could we not cast it out?" [20]And He said to them, «Because of the littleness of your faith; for truly I say to you, if you have faith as a mustard seed, you shall say to this mountain, 'Move from here to there,' and it shall move; and nothing shall be impossible to you."

Mark 1:23-27 ~ [23]And just then there was in their synagogue a man with an unclean spirit; and he cried out, [24]saying, «What do we have to do with You, Jesus of Nazareth? Have You come to destroy us? I know who You are - the Holy One of God!» [25]And Jesus rebuked him, saying, «Be quiet, and come out of him!» [26]And throwing him into convulsions, the unclean spirit cried out with a loud voice, and came out of him. [27]And they were all amazed, so that they debated among themselves, saying, «What is this? A new teaching with authority! He commands even the unclean spirits, and they obey Him.»

Mark 1:32-34 ~ [32]And when evening had come, after the sun had set, they began bringing to Him all who were ill and those who were demon-possessed. [33]And the whole city had gathered at the door. [34]And He healed many who were ill with various diseases, and cast out many demons; and He was not permitting the demons to speak, because they knew who He was.

Mark 1:39 ~ [39]And He went into their synagogues throughout all Galilee, preaching and casting out the demons.

Mark 7:25-30 ~ ²⁵But after hearing of Him, a woman whose little daughter had an unclean spirit, immediately came and fell at His feet. ²⁶Now the woman was a Gentile, of the Syrophoenician race. And she kept asking Him to cast the demon out of her daughter. ²⁷And He was saying to her, "Let the children be satisfied first, for it is not good to take the children's bread and throw it to the dogs." ²⁸But she answered and said to Him, «Yes, Lord, but even the dogs under the table feed on the children's crumbs.» ²⁹And He said to her, "Because of this answer go your way; the demon has gone out of your daughter." ³⁰And going back to her home, she found the child lying on the bed, the demon having departed.

Mark 3:10-11 ~ ¹⁰for He had healed many, with the result that all those who had afflictions pressed about Him in order to touch Him. ¹¹And whenever the unclean spirits beheld Him, they would fall down before Him and cry out, saying, "You are the Son of God!"

Mark 3:13-15 ~ ¹³And He went up to the mountain and summoned those whom He Himself wanted, and they came to Him. ¹⁴And He appointed twelve, that they might be with Him, and that He might send them out to preach, ¹⁵and to have authority to cast out the demons.

Mark 6:7 ~ And He summoned the twelve and began to send them out in pairs; and He was giving them authority over the unclean spirits;

Mark 9:20-29 ~ [20]And they brought the boy to Him. And when he saw Him, immediately the spirit threw him into a convulsion, and falling to the ground, he began rolling about and foaming at the mouth. [21]And He asked his father, "How long has this been happening to him?" And he said, "From childhood. [22]And it has often thrown him both into the fire and into the water to destroy him. But if You can do anything, take pity on us and help us!" [23]And Jesus said to him, « 'If You can!' All things are possible to him who believes.» [24]Immediately the boy's father cried out and began saying, «I do believe; help my unbelief.» [25]And when Jesus saw that a crowd was rapidly gathering, He rebuked the unclean spirit, saying to it, «You deaf and dumb spirit, I command you, come out of him and do not enter him again.» [26]And after crying out and throwing him into terrible convulsions, it came out; and the boy became so much like a corpse that most of them said, «He is dead!» [27]But Jesus took him by the hand and raised him; and he got up. [28]And when He had come into the house, His disciples began questioning Him privately, "Why could we not cast it out?" [29]And He said to them, «This kind cannot come out by anything but prayer.»

Luke 4:33-36 ~ [33]And there was a man in the synagogue possessed by the spirit of an unclean demon, and he cried out with a loud voice, [34]»Ha! What do we have to do with You, Jesus of Nazareth? Have You come to destroy us? I know who You are - the Holy One of God!» [35]And Jesus rebuked him, saying, «Be quiet and come out of him!» And when the demon had thrown him down in their midst, he came out of him without doing him any harm. [36]And amazement came upon them all, and they began discussing with one another saying, «What is this message? For with authority and power He commands the unclean spirits, and they come out.»

Luke 4:40-41 ~ [40]And while the sun was setting, all who had any sick with various diseases brought them to Him; and laying His hands on every one of them, He was healing them. [41]And demons also were coming out of many, crying out and saying, «You are the Son of God!» And rebuking them, He would not allow them to speak, because they knew Him to be the Christ.

Luke 8:27-33 ~ [27]And when He had come out onto the land, He was met by a certain man from the city who was possessed with demons; and who had not put on any clothing for a long time, and was not living in a house, but in the tombs. [28]And seeing Jesus, he cried out and fell before Him, and said in a loud voice, "What do I have to do with You, Jesus, Son of the Most High

God? I beg You, do not torment me." ²⁹For He had been commanding the unclean spirit to come out of the man. For it had seized him many times; and he was bound with chains and shackles and kept under guard; and yet he would burst his fetters and be driven by the demon into the desert. ³⁰And Jesus asked him, «What is your name?» And he said, «Legion»; for many demons had entered him. ³¹And they were entreating Him not to command them to depart into the abyss. ³²Now there was a herd of many swine feeding there on the mountain; and the demons entreated Him to permit them to enter the swine. And He gave them permission. ³³And the demons came out from the man and entered the swine; and the herd rushed down the steep bank into the lake, and were drowned.

Luke 9:37-40, 42-43a ~ ³⁷And it came about on the next days that when they had come down from the mountain, a great multitude met Him. ³⁸And behold, a man from the multitude shouted out saying, "Teacher, I beg You to look at my son, for he is my only boy, ³⁹and behold, a spirit seizes him, and he suddenly screams, and it throws him into a convulsion with foaming at the mouth, and as it mauls him, it scarcely leaves him. ⁴⁰And I begged Your disciples to cast it out, and they couldn't."... ⁴²And while he was still approaching, the demon dashed him to the ground and threw him into a convulsion. But Jesus rebuked the unclean spirit, and healed the boy, and gave him back to his father. ⁴³And they were all amazed at the greatness of God.

Luke 9:49-50 ~ ⁴⁹And John answered and said, «Master, we saw someone casting out demons in Your name; and we tried to hinder him because he does not follow along with us.» ⁵⁰But Jesus said to him, «Do not hinder him; for he who is not against you is for you.»

Luke 11:14 ~¹⁴And He was casting out a demon, and it was dumb; and it came about when the demon had gone out, the dumb man spoke; and the multitudes marvelled.

Luke 11:20 ~ ²⁰»But if I cast out demons by the finger of God, then the kingdom of God has come upon you."

As we conclude this chapter, we are not the same as we were when we started. We have navigated the terrain of faith, witnessed the authority of Christ over unclean spirits and demons, and discovered that the same power is accessible to us. Through His words and actions, Jesus has demonstrated that faith— even if as small as a mustard seed — is all it takes to move mountains, to cast out the demons that torment us, to bring light into the shadows of our existence.

The accounts across the scriptures — from the possessed man in the synagogue of Mark to the child tormented by an unclean spirit in Matthew, and from the Syrophoenician woman's plea in Mark to the astonishing authority showcased in Luke — these accounts have shown us the face of faith, the power of prayer, and the divine authority available to all who believe.

As we move forward, let us carry these lessons in our hearts: that we are not powerless in the face of our trials, that we have the God-given authority to face and cast out our inner demons, and that with faith, nothing is impossible. Let us remember the words of Jesus as we encounter our own mountains, «If you can! All things are possible to him who believes.» Let this chapter stand as a testament to God's love, the authority of Christ, and the power of unwavering faith. In God's kingdom, even the little ones can move mountains.

Remember, we are all holders of the mustard seed. Let us have faith, for the kingdom of God is within our grasp. As we step into the world, let our lives bear testimony to the power of faith, the authority over unclean spirits, and the eternal love of our Heavenly Father.

Power and Authority

In the chapters that unfold within «The Little Book that Moves the Mountains», we are setting foot on the sacred path that leads us to better understanding the divine Power and Authority emanating from the Word of God. As we embark on this journey through the chapter titled «Power and Authority», let us pause, quiet our hearts and minds, and stand in humble awe of the might and majesty of our Lord.

This chapter draws its breath from a multitude of sacred scriptures that encapsulate the immense power and authority embodied by Jesus Christ. As we delve into the depths of these verses, we will witness how Christ, bestowed with all authority in heaven and on earth (Matthew 28:18), exercised this power to heal, to command the forces of nature, and to trample the powers of darkness.

The scriptures chosen from Matthew, Mark, Luke, John, and Acts reveal the transformative power of Christ's words. These scriptures invite us to consider how, through Christ, even the seemingly insurmountable mountains in our lives can be moved. In the face of fear, we will discover that Jesus invites us to step out of our comfort zones, as Peter did onto the water (Matthew 14:28-31), trusting in His power to hold us up.

Matthew 14:36 ~ And they began to entreat Him that they might just touch the fringe of His cloak; and as many as touched it were cured.

Matthew 8:16-17 ~ [16]And when evening had come, they brought to Him many who were demon-possessed; and He cast out the spirits with a word, and healed all who were ill [17]in order that what was spoken through Isaiah the prophet might be fulfilled, saying, «HE HIMSELF TOOK OUR INFIRMITIES, AND CARRIED AWAY OUR DISEASES.»

Matthew 8:23-26 ~ [23]And when He got into the boat, His disciples followed Him. [24]And behold, there arose a great storm in the sea, so that the boat was covered with the waves; but He Himself was asleep. [25]And they came to Him, and awoke Him, saying, "Save us, Lord; we are perishing!" [26]And He said to them, «Why are you timid, you men of little faith?» Then He arose, and rebuked the winds and the sea; and it became perfectly calm.

Matthew 14:28-31 ~ [28]And Peter answered Him and said, "Lord, if it is You, command me to come to You on the water" [29]And He said, "Come!" And Peter got out of the boat, and walked on the water and came toward Jesus. [30]But seeing the wind, he became afraid, and beginning to sink, he cried out, saying, "Lord save me!" [31]And immediately Jesus stretched out His hand and took hold of him, and said to him, «O you of little faith, why did you doubt?»

Matthew 28:18 ~ And Jesus came up and spoke to them, saying, "All authority has been given to Me in heaven and on earth.

Mark 4:38-41 ~ [38]And He Himself was in the stern, asleep on the cushion; and they awoke Him and said to Him, "Teacher do You not care that we are perishing?" [39]And being aroused, He rebuked the wind and said to the sea, «Hush, be still.» And the wind died down and it became perfectly calm. [40]And He said to them, «Why are you so timid? How is it that you have no faith?» [41]And they became very much afraid and said to one another, "Who is this, that even the wind and the sea obey Him?"

Mark 6:50-52 ~ [50]For they all saw Him and were frightened. But immediately He spoke with them and said to them, "Take courage; it is I, do not be afraid." [51]And He got into the boat with them, and the wind stopped; and they were greatly astonished, [52]for they had not gained any insight from the incident of the loaves, but their heart was hardened.

Luke 4:38-39 ~ [38]And He arose and left the synagogue, and entered Simon's home. Now Simon's mother-in-law was suffering from a high fever; and they made request of Him on her behalf. [39]And standing over her, He rebuked the fever, and it left her; and she immediately arose and waited on them.

Luke 8:22-25 ~ [22]Now it came about on one of those days, that He and His disciples got into a boat, and He said to them, "Let us go over to the other side of the lake." And they launched out. [23]But as they were sailing along He fell asleep; and a fierce gale of wind descended upon the lake, and they began to be swamped and to be in danger. [24]And they came to Him and woke Him up, saying, "Master, Master, we are perishing!" And being aroused, He rebuked the wind and the surging waves, and they stopped, and it became calm. [25]And He said to them, «Where is your faith?» And they were fearful and amazed, saying to one another, «Who then is this, that He commands even the winds and the water, and they obey Him?»

Luke 10:17-20 ~ [17]And the seventy returned with joy, saying, «Lord, even the demons are subject to us in Your name.» [18]And He said to them, «I was watching Satan fall from heaven like lightning. [19]»Behold, I have given you authority to tread upon serpents and scorpions, and over all the power of the enemy, and nothing shall injure you. [20]»Nevertheless do not rejoice in this, that the spirits are subject to you, but rejoice that your names are recorded in heaven.»

John 5:21 ~ «For just as the Father raises the dead and gives them life, even so the Son also gives life to whom He wishes."

Acts 1:8 ~ But you shall receive power when the Holy Spirit has come upon you; and you shall be My witnesses both in Jerusalem, and in all Judea and Samaria, and even to the remotest part of the earth.»

Acts 4:10 ~ [10]"Let it be known to all of you, and to all the people of Israel, that by the name of Jesus Christ the Nazarene, whom you crucified, whom God raised from the dead - by this name this man stands here before you in good health."

Acts 4:33 ~ And with great power the apostles were giving witness to the resurrection of the Lord Jesus, and abundant grace was upon them all.

Acts 10:38 ~ "You know of Jesus of Nazareth, how God anointed Him with the Holy Spirit and with power, and how He went about doing good and healing all who were oppressed by the devil, for God was with Him."

Romans 1:16 ~ [16]For I am not ashamed of the gospel, for it is the power of God for salvation to everyone who believes, to the Jew first and also to the Greek. [17]For in it the righteousness of God is revealed from faith to faith; as it is written, "BUT THE RIGHTEOUS MAN SHALL LIVE BY FAITH."

Romans 4:17 ~ (as it is written, «A FATHER OF MANY NATIONS HAVE I MADE YOU») in the presence of Him whom he believed, even God, who gives life to the dead and calls into being that which does not exist.

Romans 8:11 ~ But if the Spirit of Him who raised Jesus from the dead dwells in you, He who raised Christ Jesus from the dead will also give life to your mortal bodies through His Spirit who indwells in you.

1 Corinthians 2:4-5 ~ [4]And my message and my preaching were not in persuasive words of wisdom, but in demonstration of the Spirit and of power, [5]so that your faith should not rest on the wisdom of men, but on the power of God.

1 Corinthians 4:20 ~ For the kingdom of God does not consist in words, but in power.

1 Corinthians 6:14 ~ Now God has not only raised the Lord, but will also raise us up through His power.

Ephesians 3:20-21 ~ [20]Now to Him who is able to do exceeding abundantly beyond all that we ask or think, according to the power that works within us, [21]to Him be the glory in the church and in Christ Jesus to all generations forever and ever. Amen.

Ephesians 6:12-13 ~ [12]For our struggle is not against flesh and blood, but against the rulers, against the powers, against the world forces of this darkness, against the spiritual forces of wickedness in the heavenly places. [13]Therefore, take up the full armour of God, that you may be able to resist in the evil day, and having done everything, to stand firm.

Philippians 2:8-11 ~ [8]And being found in appearances as a man, He humbled Himself by becoming obedient to the point of death, even death on a cross. [9]Therefore also God highly exalted Him, and bestowed on Him the name which is above every name, [10]that at the name of Jesus EVERY KNEE SHOULD BOW, of those who are in heaven, and on earth, and under the earth, [11]and that every tongue should confess that Jesus is Lord, to the glory of God the Father.

Colossians 3:10, 15 ~ [10]And in Him you have been made complete, and He is the head over all rule and authority;...[15]When He had disarmed the rulers and authorities, He made a public display of them, having triumphed over them through Him.

1 Thessalonians 1:5 ~ For our gospel did not come to you in word only, but also in power and in the Holy Spirit and with full conviction; just as you know what kind of men we proved to be among you for your sake.

1 Peter 2:24 ~ And He Himself bore our sins in His body on the cross, that we might die to sin and live to righteousness; for by His wounds you were healed.

1 John 3:8b ~ ...The Son of God appeared for this purpose, that He might destroy the works of the devil.

1 John 4:4 ~ You are from God, little children, and have overcome them; because greater is He who is in you than he who is in the world.

Revelation 1:17-18 ~ [17]And when I saw Him, I fell at His feet as a dead man, And He laid His right hand upon me, saying, "Do not be afraid; I am the first and the last, [18]and the living One; and I was dead, and behold, I am alive forevermore, and I have the keys of death and of Hades."

Revelation 12:11 ~ And they overcame him [the devil] because of the blood of the Lamb and because of the word of their testimony, and they did not love their life even to death.

Having journeyed through this chapter, we have witnessed, time and again, the immense power and authority Jesus holds. We've seen His mastery over nature, the power of His healing, and His dominion over the forces of darkness. In Him, the storms in our lives find their calm, and the chains of illness and oppression are broken.

In Christ, we find a power that exceeds all we can ask or think (Ephesians 3:20). His resurrection, a testament to this divine power, promises us new life, hope, and the capacity to overcome. And as the Holy Spirit works within us, we become partakers of this same divine authority, commissioned to bear witness to Christ's resurrection (Acts 1:8, 4:33).

As we close this chapter, let us carry in our hearts the empowering truth that in Christ, we have been made complete (Colossians 3:10). Through Him, we are more than conquerors, for «greater is He who is in you than he who is in the world» (1 John 4:4).

May this understanding of Christ's power and authority breathe life into our faith, inspiring us to face life's challenges not with fear but with courage and conviction, as we continue our spiritual journey through the rest of this profound book.

Word of Life / Promises

In our journey through life, we often find ourselves standing at the foot of formidable mountains—those of doubt, of fear, of uncertainty, of despair. Yet, within the Word of God, we uncover an eternal truth that resounds with faith and hope: our Father who resides in the heavens has bestowed upon us the power to move these mountains, one prayer at a time.

In this chapter, «Word of Life, Promises,» we delve into the Scriptures to shed light on God's unwavering promises for each one of us. The texts you are about to read will inspire, challenge, and fill your heart with the hope that comes from the Word of the Lord. These words, that have stood the test of time, have the power to bring life, to guide us in our darkest hours, and to remind us that we are never alone.

Our Heavenly Father longs to give good gifts to His children (Matthew 7:11), and that includes the strength to face and overcome the challenges that come our way. The teachings of Christ remind us of our potential, of the abundant life we are invited to live, and of the immeasurable power of prayer and faith.

As you embark on this journey through the Word of Life, remember: the words of Christ will never pass away (Mark 13:31; Luke 21:33). They are a beacon of hope amidst the changing tides of this world, promising us that no matter how overwhelming life's storms may seem, our God is bigger. Our God is stronger. And He is committed to bringing about justice and answering the cries of His elect (Luke 18:1-8).

May these passages of Scripture serve as a balm to your weary soul, ignite your faith, and remind you of the transforming power of God's promises.

Matthew 7:11 ~ "If you then, being evil, know how to give good gifts to your children, how much more shall your Father who is in heaven give what is good to those who ask Him!"

Mark 13:31 ~ «Heaven and earth will pass away, but My words will not pass away."

Luke 11:9-13 ~ [9]»And I say to you, ask, and it shall be given to you; seek, and you shall find; knock, and it shall be opened to you. [10]For everyone who asks, receives; and he who seeks, finds; and to him who knocks, it shall be opened. [11]Now suppose one of you fathers is asked by his son for a fish; he will not give him a snake instead of a fish, will he? [12]Or if he is asked for an egg, he will not give him a scorpion, will he? [13]If you then, being evil, know how to give good gifts to your children, how much more shall your heavenly Father give the Holy Spirit to those who ask Him?»

Luke 18:1-8 ~ [1]Now He was telling them a parable to show that at all times they ought to pray and not to lose heart, [2]saying, «There was in a certain city a judge who did not fear God and did not respect man. [3]And there was a widow in that city, and she kept coming to him, saying, 'Give me legal protection from my opponent.' [4]And for a while he was unwilling; but afterward he said to himself, 'Even though I do not fear God nor respect man, [5]yet because this widow bothers me, I will give her legal protection, lest by continually coming she wear me out.'» [6]And the Lord said, «Hear what the unrighteous judge said; [7]now, shall not God bring about justice for His elect, who cry to Him day and night, and will He delay long over them? [8]I tell you that He will bring about justice for them speedily. However, when the Son of Man comes, will He find faith on the earth?»

Luke 18:27 ~ But He said, «The things impossible with men are possible with God.»

Luke 21:33 ~ «Heaven and earth will pass away, but My words will not pass away.

John 1:4 ~ In Him was life, and the life was the Light of men.

John 10:10 ~ ¹⁰»The thief comes only to steal, and kill, and destroy; I came that they might have life, and might have it abundantly."

John 10:37-38 ~ ³⁷»If I do not do the works of My Father, do not believe Me; ³⁸but if I do them, though you do not believe Me, believe the works, that you may know and understand that the Father is in Me, and I in the Father.»

John 12:31-32 ~ «Now judgment is upon this world; now the ruler of this world shall be cast out. ³²And I, if I be lifted up from the earth, will draw all men to Myself."

John 14:12-14 ~ ¹²»Truly, truly, I say to you, he who believes in Me, the works that I do shall he do also; and greater works than these shall he do; because I go to the Father. ¹³And whatever you ask in My name, that will I do, so that the Father may be glorified in the Son. ¹⁴If you ask Me anything in My name, I will do it."

John 15:16 ~ ¹⁶»You did not choose Me, but I chose you, and appointed you, that you should go and bear fruit, and that your fruit should remain, that whatever you ask of the Father in My name, He may give to you."

John 16:23-24 ~ [23]»And in that day you will ask Me no question. Truly, truly, I say to you, if you shall ask the Father for anything, He will give it to you in My name. [24]Until now you have asked for nothing in My name; ask and you will receive, that your joy may be made full."

2 Corinthians 1:20 ~ For as many as may be the promises of God, in Him they are yes; wherefore also by Him is our Amen to the glory of God through us.

2 Corinthians 5:17 ~ Therefore if any man is in Christ, he is a new creature; the old things passed away; behold, new things have come.

Galatians 3:13-14, 29 ~ [13]Christ redeemed us from the curse of the Law, having become a curse for us - for it is written, "CURSED IS EVERYONE WHO HANGS ON A TREE" - [14]in order that in Christ Jesus the blessing of Abraham might come to the Gentiles, so that we might receive the promise if the Spirit through faith...[29]And if you belong to Christ, then you are Abraham's offspring, heirs according to the promise.

Ephesians 2:5-6 ~ [5]Even when we were dead in our transgressions, made us alive together with Christ (by grace you have been saved), [6]and raised us up with Him, and seated us with Him in the heavenly places in Christ Jesus.

Ephesians 4:24 ~ And put on the new self, which in the likeness of God has been created in righteousness and holiness of the truth.

Ephesians 5:8 ~ For you were formerly darkness, but now you are light in the Lord; walk as children of light.

Ephesians 6:10 ~ Finally, be strong in the Lord, and in the strength of His might.

Philippians 1:6 ~ For I am confident of this very thing, that He who began a good work in you will perfect it until the day of Christ Jesus.

Colossians 1:13-14 ~ [13]For He delivered us from the domain of darkness, and transferred us to the kingdom of His beloved Son, [14]In whom we have redemption, the forgiveness of sins.

1 Thessalonians 5:23 ~ Now may the God of peace Himself sanctify you entirely; and may your spirit and soul and body be preserved complete, without blame at the coming of our Lord Jesus Christ.

Hebrews 6:11-12 ~ ¹¹And we desire that each one of you show the same diligence so as to realize the full assurance of hope until the end, ¹²that you may not be sluggish, but imitators of those who through faith and patience inherit the promises.

Hebrews 13:8 ~ Jesus Christ is the same yesterday and today, yes and forever.

Hebrews 12:12-13 ~ ¹²Therefore, strengthen the hands that are weak and the knees that are feeble, ¹³and make straight paths for your feet, so that the limb which is lame may not be put out of joint, but rather be healed.

James 4:7 ~ Submit therefore to God. Resist the devil and he will flee from you.

2 Peter 1:3-4a ~ ³Seeing that His divine power has granted to us everything pertaining to life and godliness, through the true knowledge of Him who called us by His own glory and excellence. ⁴For by these He has granted to us His precious and magnificent promises, in order that by them you might become partakers of the divine nature.

1 John 4:14 ~ And we have beheld and bear witness that the Father has sent the Son to be the Saviour of the World.

Dear reader, as we conclude our journey through this chapter, «Word of Life, Promises,» we find ourselves standing not at the foot, but at the peak of these mountains. We have not only ventured into, but also tasted the depths of God's promises—promises that assure us of His unending love, grace, and commitment to us.

Throughout these Scriptures, we see a loving Father who gives good gifts (Luke 11:9-13), a Savior who came so we might have life abundantly (John 10:10), and a divine power that has granted to us everything pertaining to life and godliness (2 Peter 1:3-4a).

We have been reminded that we are new creatures in Christ (2 Corinthians 5:17), that we have been redeemed from the curse of the Law (Galatians 3:13-14), and that we are heirs of Abraham's promise through faith (Galatians 3:29). We have discovered that the things impossible with men are possible with God (Luke 18:27).

In Him, we find a firm foundation on which to stand, an anchor for our souls, and the assurance that He who began a good work in us will perfect it until the day of Christ Jesus (Philippians 1:6).

So let us not lose heart, but rather, let us go forth with a strengthened resolve, reassured by the words of life that His promises are indeed yes and Amen (2 Corinthians 1:20). Let us continue to ask, to seek, and to knock, knowing that our loving Father hears us and answers us according to His perfect will. Let us cling tightly to these promises, living as children of light (Ephesians 5:8) and bearers of His life-giving Word. For in Him, we find not only comfort and healing, but also the promise of life eternal (1 John 4:14).

As we move forward, may we hold fast to these truths, letting them guide us as we continue our journey through «The Little Book that Moves the Mountains.»

Conclusion

As we close the final pages of «The Little Book that Moves the Mountains,» we find ourselves standing on the crest of the final summit, looking back over the journey we have taken together. We have delved deeply into the abundant promises of God, explored the transformative power of prayer, and embraced the realities of faith that empowers us to move mountains in our lives.

From understanding the Word of Life and its promises to recognizing the power of persistent prayer and the significance of unyielding faith, we have navigated a path that illuminated the vast landscape of God's love and grace. The truths we have discovered are not merely words on a page but are divine promises that echo across time, shaping our hearts and guiding our steps toward a life firmly grounded in Christ.

Reflect upon the lessons learned from the enduring teachings of Christ, and recall the invaluable wisdom drawn from the wells of Scripture. The image of our Heavenly Father, who showers good gifts upon His children (Matthew 7:11) and the reassurance that with Him, the impossible becomes possible (Luke 18:27) are not mere platitudes but divine realities that inform our lives.

As we journeyed through each chapter, we were continually reminded of the transformation that occurs when we fully embrace the truth of Christ in our lives: we become new creations (2 Corinthians 5:17), redeemed and adopted into God's eternal family (Galatians 3:13-14, 29). We were also challenged to be strong in the Lord, and in the strength of His might (Ephesians 6:10), recognizing that our Father in Heaven is not just a distant deity but an ever-present help and source of unending strength.

Remember the promise of Jesus, who declared that the thief comes only to steal, kill, and destroy, but He came that we might have life, and have it abundantly (John 10:10). With these words echoing in our hearts, we can face each new day, not with fear, but with the certainty of God's abiding presence and His infinite love for us.

Yet, as we stand on this summit, let us not forget that our journey is not ending but merely shifting into a new phase. For the truths we have gleaned from this book are not meant to be stored away but lived out in our everyday lives. Like the Apostle Paul, we are encouraged to «press on toward the goal for the prize of the upward call of God in Christ Jesus» (Philippians 3:14).

Our journey through «The Little Book that Moves the Mountains» has been one of exploration and discovery, of being inspired, challenged, comforted, and empowered by the unchanging Word of God. As we close this book, may the words we've studied and the truths we've unearthed continue to resonate within us, transforming our hearts, illuminating our paths, and moving the mountains that stand in our way.

May you step out in faith, secure in the knowledge that God is with you, that His promises are steadfast, and that He is working in you to achieve His good purpose. May the journey we have taken through the pages of this book serve as a launching point for a deeper, more intimate walk with God—a journey that truly moves mountains.

Connect With Us

As you journey through life, it is essential to remember that you are not alone. We understand that spiritual growth and the quest for understanding are ongoing processes that often raise questions, and we are here to support you as you navigate through these inquiries. We are passionate about providing valuable resources, teachings, and fostering a community of individuals who are earnestly seeking a deeper relationship with God.

1. Visit our Website: Delve deeper into your spiritual journey by visiting the History Makers Academy website at https://historymakersacademy.com/. Our website offers a wealth of resources, from additional readings to online courses, aimed at helping you grow in your walk with God.

2. Join our YouTube Channel: Tune into our YouTube channel, @HistoryMakersTV805, for insightful teachings and uplifting messages that will encourage and inspire you in your spiritual walk. Our videos are designed to help you understand and apply God's Word to your everyday life, strengthening your relationship

with Him and empowering you to become a history maker in your own right.

3. Connect via Email: We value your thoughts, questions, and insights. Feel free to reach out to us at admin@historymakersacademy.com with any inquiries or feedback. Whether you're seeking guidance on a particular topic, want to share your testimonies or need prayer, we're here for you.

Remember, your spiritual journey is not meant to be a solitary pursuit. We at History Makers Academy are dedicated to walking alongside you, offering guidance, support, and a community rooted in faith. Don't hesitate to reach out; we're here to serve and support you in your walk with God. Together, we can move mountains.

Manufactured by Amazon.ca
Bolton, ON

34707020R00057